Lifelines 8

Robert Stephenson

An illustrated life of
Robert Stephenson

1803-1859

Donald J. Smith

Shire Publications Ltd.

Contents

ACKNOWLEDGEMENTS

The author and publishers wish to thank the following for permission to reproduce the illustrations on the pages indicated: Alfred E. Bristow 2; The Science Museum, London 4, 10, 15, 21, 39 (lower), 43; The Radio Times Hulton Picture Library 9, 34; The Museum of British Transport, Clapham, London 18; Keith Bennett 41; Greater Manchester Museum of Science and Industry 46.

Copyright © 1973 by Donald J. Smith. First published 1973; reprinted 1980 and 1984. ISBN 0 85263 186 3.

Printed in Great Britain by C. I. Thomas & Sons (Haverfordwest) Ltd, Press Buildings, Merlins Bridge, Haverfordwest.

Opposite: This statue of Robert Stephenson, by Baron Marochetti, was erected in the forecourt of Euston Station, the London terminus of Stephenson's London to Birmingham Railway.

Father and son

EARLY LIFE

It is remarkable how the genius of Robert Stephenson, one of the greatest railway and civil engineers of the nineteenth century, has been overshadowed by the reputation of his even more celebrated father. This is not to detract from the fame of George Stephenson, but a comment on the becoming modesty of a son who equalled in flair, while surpassing in intellect, the father whose fame owes more to time and opportunity than to depth of knowledge or understanding.

Robert was born on 16th November 1803 in a riverside cottage at Willington Quay near Newcastle-on-Tyne, where his father was in charge of a winding engine connected with the discharge of ballast from coasting vessels. This was twelve months after George's marriage to Fanny Henderson, the daughter of a local farmer, in November 1802.

George appears to have been a restless, ambitious man, always seeking to better himself. At Willington he spent much of his spare time cleaning and repairing clocks, rendering a useful service to local pitmen who depended so much, in their shift work, on an efficient timepiece. During the autumn of 1804 he moved to Killingworth where he was employed as brakesman, and later as enginewright, at the West Moor Pit of the 'Grand Allies', then the most prosperous mining company in the North-east.

George and Fanny were a devoted couple but their happiness was short lived. In July 1805, less than a year after moving to Killingworth, Fanny gave birth to their second child, a daughter named after her. The baby died after three weeks while the

Opposite: John Lucas's painting of the Stephenson family was commissioned in 1857. It depicts George's parents (standing), his two wives (seated), George with the miner's safety lamp he invented, and Robert (with pipe). In the background is the Stephenson cottage at Killingworth, the colliery and a representation of one of George's early engines. The young girl, held by Robert's mother, is George's daughter who died in childhood.

5

mother, weakened by childbirth, sickened of consumption and died on 14th May 1806.

George was in despair and felt he must free himself of unhappy memories—if only for a short while—by giving up his job and escaping from the district. Leaving his three-year-old son in the care of a housekeeper he tramped northwards, eventually finding work in charge of steam engines at a spinning mill in Montrose, Scotland. It was over twelve months before he returned to Killingworth, being completely cut off from family and friends throughout this period. It must have been a great shock to find his once familiar cottage locked and shuttered, as though long deserted. During his absence the housekeeper had married George's brother Robert, who had taken the boy into his own home and considered adopting him. Yet George would not be separated from his son a day longer and soon engaged another housekeeper. The arrangement did not work out and young Robert was finally cared for by Eleanor Stephenson—or 'Aunt Nelly'—who acted the role of foster mother to perfection.

Robert grew from a sickly child into a slim, wiry schoolboy, mainly due to the care of his devoted aunt. He was troubled in early life by a lung weakness but had enough of his father's side to make him both energetic and resilient. From an early age he showed a keenness for books unknown to his father, who although attending night school in young manhood, was sadly lacking in formal education. Yet despite his ignorance the older man could at least sense the value of reading habits. He paid a keen interest in Robert's progress, sending him to study under a schoolmaster at Longbenton, two miles from Killingworth, almost as soon as the boy could walk. George was a devoted father but might have proved a hard taskmaster without the intervention and thoughtfulness of a watchful aunt.

After school hours the boy was expected to run errands for his father and read extracts from the papers and technical books the older man could not have tackled without difficulty. Yet Robert was deeply fond of his father, holding him in both affection and respect, although often sorely tried by George's bluntness of manner. It was understood, even before he started school, that Robert would train to become an engineer and join his father in a working partnership. In the meantime he was crammed to the limits of his intellect and, by the age of twelve, had absorbed all he could be taught by local men.

George Stephenson.

The Stephensons' cottage at Killingworth.

Instead of sending his son to a grammar school George chose a private academy in Percy Street, Newcastle-on-Tyne, run by a Dr Bruce. This was a school patronised by the professional classes, where Robert acquired an air of polish to complement his natural charm of manner. Newcastle was ten miles from Killingworth and as this was too far to walk in both directions, he was given a donkey or 'cuddy' and ambled to school at an easy gait, often reading as he rode. Robert remained at Percy Street for nearly four years, leaving school at the age of sixteen.

KILLINGWORTH AND AFTER

In 1819 Robert was apprenticed by his father to Nicholas Wood, the head coal-viewer at Killingworth Colliery. This meant long hours of underground work, involving great risk to life and limb. Robert's health began to deteriorate and in 1821 he left the pit to attend a course of science lectures at Edinburgh University. In the meantime his father had been experimenting with colliery railways both at Killingworth and at Hetton, establishing a reputation for knowledge of locomotives and layout of tracks. He was soon involved in making surveys for the newly projected Stockton and Darlington Railway and gave Robert the opportunity to join him, not merely as an assistant, but as a fully fledged partner. Robert's name appeared on the contract, at his father's request, as a qualified engineer and attempts by certain biographers to make him seem a mere apprentice have long been disproved. The part of the railway known as the 'Haggar Leases Branch' was delegated entirely to young Robert Stephenson who was responsible for surveying and engineering this section throughout. He also designed stationary haulage engines used on part of the main line.

Robert later assisted his father in surveying the Liverpool and Manchester Railway, but found this less rewarding than similar work in the Durham coalfields, owing to the hostility of the Lancashire farmers, landowners and workpeople, many of whom tried to thwart his efforts with both threats and acts of violence. The head of the survey team, under the aegis of George Stephenson, was William James, a Warwickshire engineer and land agent, who had involved himself in the promotion of railways with the enthusiasm of a convert to a new religion. It was mainly due to the inspiration and fortitude of William James that the survey party completed their work by 4th

The ruins of Killingworth High Pit, as engraved for the 'Illustrated London News' in 1881.

October 1822, the only part in which the chain men were not molested being the bog of Chat Moss, where even local farmers feared to wander alone. Robert Stephenson greatly admired the courage and will-power of William James, the memory of which served him as a pattern of conduct in later life.

During 1823 Robert Stephenson accompanied his father on a tour of the British Isles, partly concerned with the installation of machinery and partly to survey some of the more outstanding engineering and architectural works then extant. While in London they investigated the claims of Jacob Perkins, an American inventor, who was said to have constructed a high-pressure steam engine superior to any yet made. This was supposed to be so powerful that no single man could stop the machinery once it was set in motion. George Stephenson was bold enough to expose this as a fraud by stopping the flywheel with one hand, proving it to be only of four horse-power, despite advertisements that it was more than double the strength.

ROBERT STEPHENSON AND COMPANY

Returning to the north George Stephenson decided to open an engineering works that would provide him with the locomotives and equipment needed in his various railway schemes. Edward Pease, one of the founders of the Stockton and Darlington company, along with a Mr Richardson and a Mr Longridge, were persuaded to invest money in the undertaking which was to be superintended by Robert Stephenson. This was to become 'Robert Stephenson and Company', of the celebrated Forth Street works, and first of the world's great locomotive construction plants.

As well as being a business partner and representing his father's interest—George preferring to keep in the background—Robert was to be his own designer, draughtsman, works manager and accountant, the first contract being to supply locomotives for the Stockton and Darlington line—forty miles from Newcastle. This was being 'thrown in at the deep end' and the strain of his new responsibilities seems to have caused a relapse in Robert's health. On the business side alone Robert was almost entirely lacking in experience, while equipment of the works—during the early days—was primitive even by pioneer standards. It is greatly to his credit that he kept the works running at a high pitch of efficiency for even a short period and not surprising that he should seize the first opportunity to leave Forth Street by joining a mining enterprise in South America, where it was thought the warmer climate might also restore his health.

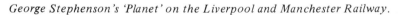

George Stephenson's 'Planet' on the Liverpool and Manchester Railway.

The first railways

THE SOUTH AMERICAN VENTURE

Robert Stephenson was recommended to take charge of operations at the Santa Ana mines, near Mariquita in the Colombian Andes, by the financier Thomas Richardson, who was a friend of Edward Pease and had invested money in both the Colombian enterprise and the Forth Street works. He had been greatly impressed by the engineering skill of Robert Stephenson, whom he had consulted over the purchase of equipment. Robert signed on for a period of three years at a salary of £500 per annum, then a princely sum for a young man. While sorry to disappoint his father and leave his friends, the rich promise of South America attracted him beyond discretion.

The climate of the country and the situation of the mines proved to be all Robert might have wished for. The scenery was beautiful, the mountain air pure, the natives friendly and the living cheap. While a house was being built for him he lodged in the cottage of the local priest, spending much of his spare time in reading and study. When tiring of his own company he was made welcome in the best society of the capital, Bogota. The great shock came when he had to bring to order a gang of headstrong Cornish miners, sent from the homeland to replace native labour. Although hand-picked for their mining skill the Cornishmen were brutal and clannish, given to free fights and wild drinking bouts that shocked even the local people. They were unwilling to take orders from a younger man and sure that none but their own people really understood the secrets of mining. It may be noted that before going out to Colombia Robert had spent some time as an observer in the Cornish tin mines.

At one stage the Cornishmen plotted a mutiny and kept Robert awake with their loud ribaldry and shouted threats. It was only by displaying the same brand of coolness with which William James had faced the Lancashire rabble that he was able to withstand them. Little did they suspect the uneasy feelings of the naturally pale young man, who lounged on his doorstep smoking a cigar, seeming nonchalant to the point of arrogance. They were too drunk to do him serious harm but Robert later narrowed the gap between them by challenging their leaders to feats of skill and endurance in which they normally revelled when sober. He soon mastered the art of throwing quoits, one of their favourite pastimes, and abandoned books in favour of boyish games such as their ancestors might have played on village greens for centuries past. Yet despite improved labour relations, work in South America became increasingly difficult. The Spanish colonists had worked the mines until recent years only through the use of slave labour. It was impossible to show reasonable profits when the new company over-paid a feckless crew to do the work of subservient natives. Costly mining machinery sent from Europe was often too cumbersome to transport on the backs of mules over rough tracks of the interior and was left to rust where it had been landed. The advice and instructions concerning these matters sent back by Robert Stephenson was ignored or countermanded. By the end of three years he was eager enough to return to the comparative peace and sanity of his native Northumbria.

Before returning from South America Robert experienced a chance encounter with the engineer Richard Trevithick. They met in a tavern at the port of Cartagena—Trevithick, inventor of the railway locomotive, once the friend of rulers and statesmen, ruined by speculation and failure in the mines of South America. Now an old man with failing health and broken spirit he was ready to return to his native Cornwall, glad to accept enough money from Robert to buy his passage home.

Although an engineer by inclination and training Robert Stephenson was also a keen observer of nature, with a great fondness for animals. While staying in South America he seemed to have acquired a small private zoo, with five monkeys, a number of parrots and other tropical birds. These were not merely exhibits, but pets which he taught tricks and lavished great affection on. His favourite was an ancient mule named Hurry, who appears to have been house-trained, and who came to the dinner table each evening—at the ringing of a bell—to be fed on a small loaf of bread. An accomplished horseman Robert was able to spend long hours in the saddle, on survey work,

The sites of the main British engineering work in which Robert
Stephenson was involved.

without fatigue.

VISIT TO NORTH AMERICA

`After leaving Colombia, before returning to England, Robert Stephenson decided to visit North America, having planned a walking tour of the eastern United States. This proved to be an exciting voyage, not without its share of horror and wretchedness. Near the islands of the West Indies they were becalmed for several days but managed to pick up the survivors of a wreck, whose own vessel had foundered in a hurricane many miles distant. The starving seamen, naked and helpless, had to be lifted on to the deck of the rescue ship by means of ropes and cradles. They had kept alive in two boats only by eating the dead bodies of their former comrades.

A short distance from New York the ship in which Robert was a passenger was struck by a great storm. Dismasted and without a stitch of canvas it was driven between huge rocks and ran aground about midnight. The storm was so rough that the hull began to break up within a few minutes, passengers and crew being in danger of their lives. Although Robert was able to come safely ashore he lost all his money and baggage, arriving with only the clothes he wore.

Having obtained money from home through a credit scheme Robert and three of his companions, all young Englishmen on their way home from South America, set out to see the sights. After a few days in town they decided to move up country, following the course of the Hudson River towards the Canadian border. Their trek of five hundred miles, mainly on foot, took them to Montreal, stopping for a short time to view the Niagara Falls. Robert seems to have formed a highly favourable opinion of the country dwellers and pioneers, who frequently offered them free bed and board, but felt less sympathy for the town folk. Of the citizens of New York he wrote: 'Outward appearances of things and persons were indicative of English manners and customs; but on closer investigation we soon discovered the characteristic impudence of the people.' Yet while the inhabitants of the United States were often brash and boastful Robert was bound to acknowledge their industry and enterprise, which found an enthusiastic response in his own attitudes.

The 'Invicta' was the first steam locomotive designed and constructed at the Stephensons' Forth Street works at Newcastle.

THE CANTERBURY AND WHITSTABLE RAILWAY

Robert now returned to the management of the Forth Street works, where he intended to revive the flagging trade of the firm, neglected in his absence. He was also appointed engineer to the Canterbury and Whitstable Railway project, but settled his working headquarters in Newcastle with frequent visits to Canterbury and London.

The Canterbury and Whitstable was a short line south of the Thames claiming to have had the first regular passenger services hauled by steam locomotives, although of its six-mile length the first four were traversed in carriages hauled by fixed engines of a type later appearing on the Church Street incline at Whitstable. The opening of the Canterbury and Whitstable was on 30th May 1830, nearly four months before the opening of the Liverpool and Manchester line. The first steam locomotive brought into service, designed and constructed at Forth Street, had four-coupled wheels of equal size and forward inclined cylinders. It was known as *Invicta* (the county motto of Kent) and was delivered by sea from Newcastle-on-Tyne to Whitstable harbour.

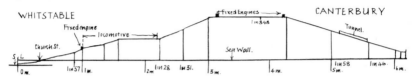

Profile of the Canterbury and Whitstable Railway.

IMPROVED LOCOMOTIVES

It was now Robert Stephenson's ambition to create a truly competitive railway locomotive that would be both lighter and faster than its predecessors. With the introduction of passenger services there was less need for a mobile beam engine capable of dragging coal trucks at little more than walking pace. The tradition of the northern counties, then with a monopoly in the use and building of railway locomotives, had been to construct cumbersome, unsightly machines, although in the south such men as Gurney had managed to harness lighter steam engines to road carriages and stage-coaches for express services. The resulting locomotive built by Robert Stephenson, after consultations with his father and examination of numerous other designs, was an improved type known as *The Lancashire Witch*, first ordered for the Liverpool and Manchester company, but later sold to the newly completed Bolton and Leigh Railway. This was a four-coupled design with sprung axles and backward inclined cylinders. A rotary plug valve in the steam pipe was geared to the rear axle and controlled steam with a variable cut off. *Lancashire Witch* was the forerunner of numerous locomotives built on the same principles at Forth Street, including the famous *Rocket* which won the Rainhill

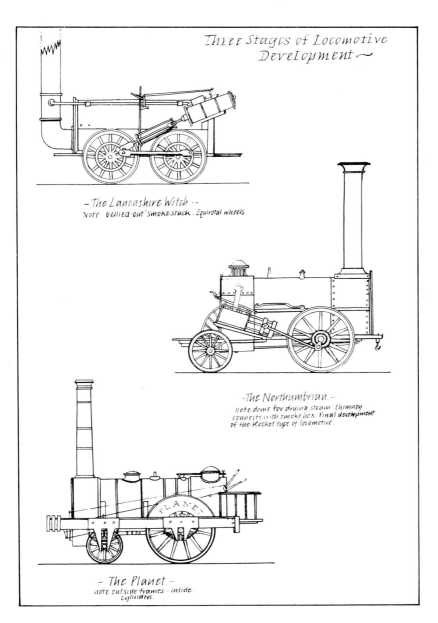

Three Stages of Locomotive Development ~

—The Lancashire Witch —
Note 'bellied-out' smoke-stack. Equirotal wheels.

—The Northumbrian.—
note dome for drying steam. Chimney connects with smoke box. Final development of the Rocket type of locomotive.

— The Planet.—
note outside frames - inside cylinders.

17

1829.

GRAND COMPETITION

OF

LOCOMOTIVES

ON THE

LIVERPOOL & MANCHESTER RAILWAY.

STIPULATIONS & CONDITIONS

ON WHICH THE DIRECTORS OF THE LIVERPOOL AND MANCHESTER RAILWAY OFFER A PREMIUM OF £500 FOR THE MOST IMPROVED LOCOMOTIVE ENGINE.

I.

The said Engine must "effectually consume its own smoke," according to the provisions of the Railway Act, 7th Geo. IV.

II.

The Engine, if it weighs Six Tons, must be capable of drawing after it, day by day, on a well-constructed Railway, on a level plane, a Train of Carriages of the gross weight of Twenty Tons, including the Tender and Water Tank, at the rate of Ten Miles per Hour, with a pressure of steam in the boiler not exceeding Fifty Pounds on the square inch.

III.

There must be Two Safety Valves, one of which must be completely out of the reach or control of the Engine-man, and neither of which must be fastened down while the Engine is working.

IV.

The Engine and Boiler must be supported on Springs, and rest on Six Wheels; and the height from the ground to the top of the Chimney must not exceed Fifteen Feet.

V.

The weight of the Machine, WITH ITS COMPLEMENT OF WATER in the Boiler, must, at most, not exceed Six Tons, and a Machine of less weight will be preferred if it draw AFTER it a PROPORTIONATE weight; and if the weight of the Engine, &c., do not exceed Five Tons, then the gross weight to be drawn need not exceed Fifteen Tons; and in that proportion for Machines of still smaller weight — provided that the Engine, &c., shall still be on six wheels, unless the weight (as above) be reduced to Four Tons and a Half, or under, in which case the Boiler, &c., may be placed on four wheels. And the Company shall be at liberty to put the Boiler, Fire Tube, Cylinders, &c., to the test of a pressure of water not exceeding 150 Pounds per square inch, without being answerable for any damage the Machine may receive in consequence.

VI.

There must be a Mercurial Gauge affixed to the Machine, with Index Rod, showing the Steam Pressure above 45 Pounds per square inch; and constructed to blow out a Pressure of 60 Pounds per inch.

VII.

The Engine to be delivered complete for trial, at the Liverpool end of the Railway, not later than the 1st of October next.

VIII.

The price of the Engine which may be accepted, not to exceed £550, delivered on the Railway; and any Engine not approved to be taken back by the Owner.

N.B.— The Railway Company will provide the ENGINE TENDER with a supply of Water and Fuel, for the experiment. The distance within the Rails is four feet eight inches and a half.

THE LOCOMOTIVE STEAM ENGINES,

WHICH COMPETED FOR THE PRIZE OF £500 OFFERED BY THE DIRECTORS OF THE LIVERPOOL AND MANCHESTER RAILWAY COMPANY.

DRAWN TO A SCALE ½ INCH TO A FOOT.

THE "ROCKET" OF Mr ROBt STEPHENSON OF NEWCASTLE.

WHICH DRAWING A LOAD EQUIVALENT TO THREE TIMES ITS WEIGHT TRAVELLED AT THE RATE OF 12½ MILES AN HOUR, AND WITH A CARRIAGE & PASSENGERS AT THE RATE OF 24 MILES. COST PER MILE FOR FUEL ABOUT THREE HALFPENCE.

THE "NOVELTY" OF MESSrs BRAITHWAITE & ERRICSSON OF LONDON.

WHICH DRAWING A LOAD EQUIVALENT TO THREE TIMES ITS WEIGHT TRAVELLED AT THE RATE OF 20¾ MILES AN HOUR, AND WITH A CARRIAGE & PASSENGERS AT THE RATE OF 32 MILES. COST PER MILE FOR FUEL ABOUT ONE HALFPENNY.

THE "SANSPAREIL" OF Mr HACKWORTH OF DARLINGTON.

WHICH DRAWING A LOAD EQUIVALENT TO THREE TIMES ITS WEIGHT TRAVELLED AT THE RATE OF 13½ MILES AN HOUR. COST FOR FUEL PER MILE ABOUT TWO PENCE.

Trials and ensured the future of steam locomotive haulage
throughout the world.

Posterity has come to regard the *Rocket* as the design solely
of George Stephenson, the 'Father of Railways'. However, both
Stephensons were involved and they were also greatly assisted
by the collaboration of Henry Booth, who was instrumental in
designing the unique multi-tubular boiler. Booth, then serving as
treasurer to the Liverpool and Manchester Railway, was in those
days a theorist rather than a practical man, although later
becoming an engineer in his own right. His idea was translated
from an inspired notion to a sound proposition by Robert
Stephenson. *The Lancashire Witch* and other locomotives of
that type had two large flues with a firebox for each. In the
Rocket or 'premium design' these were replaced by a number of
narrow-gauge tubes drawing heat from a single and separate
firebox, greatly improving the heating surface which proved the
secret of successful steaming.

The *Rocket* with its twenty-five narrow copper tubes had, in
many respects, the prototype of the modern locomotive boiler.
A dome athwart the boiler barrel was used for drying steam,
while the exhaust was directed into the chimney through two
blast pipes slightly smaller than the exhaust apertures.

One of the great difficulties encountered in the design of the
multi-tubular boiler of the *Rocket* was fixing the tubes within
the tube-plates, so that they would be both steam-proof and
secure. After an unsuccessful attempt to hold the tubes by
means of large nuts there were further experiments with
riveting. In a letter dated 21st August Robert Stephenson
described this second and more enterprising attempt, and also
how he soon hoped to give the boiler its first hydraulic tests.
Unfortunately the tube-plates tended to bulge outwards when
under pressure, splitting the sealed ends. Tube-plates had been
made as light as possible to save weight, but this weakened the
apertures for the pipes. The solution was to fit a number of
inner rods or stays between the plates which might withstand a
test pressure of 150 pounds.

In a letter to Booth dated 5th September, Robert Stephenson
described the initial tests and trial run, '... The fire burns

*Opposite: Runners at the Rainhill Trials in 1829: the 'Rocket', the
'Novelty' and the 'Sans Pareil'.*

admirably and an abundance of steam is raised when the fire is carefully attended to . . . we started from Killingworth Pit with five waggons each weighing four tuns [tons]. Add to this the tender and 40 men, we proceeded up an ascent of 11 or 12 feet per mile at 8 miles per hour . . . We went 3 miles on this railway, the rate of ascents and descents my father knows—on a level part laid with malleable iron rails, we attained a speed of 12 miles per hour and, without thinking that I deceived myself—I believe the steam did not sink on this part. On the whole the engine is capable of doing as much if not more than set forth in the stipulations.' The engine weight was 4 tons 5 hundredweights 1 quarter in working order.

On 12th September 1829 the *Rocket,* having undergone tests on the Killingworth Railway, was dismantled and taken to Carlisle for transhipment to Liverpool by sea. It performed at Rainhill on 1st October, in competition with five other machines, all of which it could have run into the ground. The *Novelty* of Braithwaite and Erickson and the *Sans Pareil* of Hackworth were its only serious rivals, both of these failing on the day of the trials through mechanical faults.

A whole string of improved locomotives was soon leaving the Forth Street works, as a result of experience gained with the *Rocket.* Cylinders were greatly enlarged and the number of boiler tubes increased while smokeboxes replaced the 'bellied-out' smoke stacks of earlier designs. The *Northumbrian,* produced for the opening of the Liverpool and Manchester line, had a boiler with 132 tubes of $1\frac{5}{8}$ inches diameter, which represented 379 square feet of heating surface. Its firebox was integral with the boiler while it drew an iron tender with coal rails rather than a mere wooden truck with water barrel and fuel space. Following the *Northumbrian* came the *Planet,* similar to contemporary steam locomotives in most respects but its lack of a modern reversible gear.

The development of the steam locomotive was by no means the sole preoccupation of Robert Stephenson. During his work on the Canterbury and Whitstable line he found time to court his future wife Fanny Sanderson, the attractive daughter of a City merchant, at whose house he had been entertained before sailing to South America. They were married at Bishopsgate parish church during the summer of 1829, and settled in a new house at Greenfield Place, Newcastle, later moving to London.

The running times of the 'Rocket' on 8th October 1829 at Rainhill as recorded in Rastrick's notebook.

In character Robert Stephenson was a mass of contradictions. Although outwardly modest and disliking public appearances, he was also obstinate to the point of fanaticism. It is said that during a dinner to celebrate the opening of the Canterbury line he was so shy as to be almost inaudible, speaking in such a low voice that trained pressmen were unable to understand him. Yet the nervous exterior concealed an iron will with great coolness in both speech and decision making. In the witness box or before a parliamentary committee he showed such skill in argument that even professional counsel respected his pleading.

EARLY RAILWAY CONTRACTS

Shortly after the opening of the Canterbury and Whitstable line Robert Stephenson was responsible for work on three small but important railways: a five-mile branch of the Bolton and Leigh Railway; a five-mile branch of the Liverpool and Manchester Railway known as the Warrington and Newton Railway; and the Leicester and Swannington system.

The Leicester and Swannington line was constructed to serve collieries in west Leicestershire in competition with the Nottinghamshire coalfield. The coal owners were desirous that a line should be laid between their pitheads and the city of Leicester, this being the result of a visit made by a director of the Long Lane Colliery Company to the Stockton and Darlington Railway in 1828. Robert Stephenson was appointed engineer to the line, having first visited the site in February 1829. The main engineering work was a tunnel nearly a mile long at Glenfield, which greatly increased expenditure and led to the accidental death of the contractor, Daniel Jowett, who fell into a shaft used in sinking the headings. The first locomotive to run on the line proved to be under-powered and a larger, more powerful version was supplied towards the end of 1833. This was known as *Atlas*, the first locomotive to run with steam brakes, recently patented at the Forth Street works. Fixed engines were used on inclined planes at Bagworth and Swannington.

The Leicester and Swannington Railway is important for two main reasons. Firstly, it became the oldest constituent line of the Midland Railway Company and thus an integral part of one of the most important systems in the country. Secondly, it was in connection with this work that Robert Stephenson surveyed the locality and founded a new mining company, which exploited untapped seams of the Leicestershire coalfield using highly efficient Northumbrian methods, superior to any then used in the East Midlands. This turned out to be one of the most profitable concerns ever undertaken by either of the Stephensons.

The trunk routes

THE GRAND JUNCTION RAILWAY

By the early 1830s various engineers and speculators were thinking in terms of a national railway system linking the main cities and ports of England. A flying survey for routes between London, Liverpool and Birmingham, which might eventually join together, had been made as early as 1825. In 1829 directors of the Warrington and Newton Railway approached Robert Stephenson with the idea of extending their line southwards to Sandbach in Cheshire—and thence to the Midland plain—through territory owned by the Marquess of Stafford. The Marquess opposed the first draft of this scheme and to avoid upsetting his father through connections with the Liverpool and Manchester Railway—pledged to support claims of the Marquess—Robert chose an alternative route via Crewe Park, where a town was later built which became one of the largest railway centres in the world. The final survey for the line between Liverpool and Birmingham was delegated to Joseph Lock, to be surveyed as far as Runcorn by Charles Vignoles—the inventor of the flat-bottomed rail named after him. This became known as 'The Grand Junction Railway', the first great trunk route in the world. It was engineered partly by Joseph Lock and partly by George Stephenson—divided into two contracts—although Lock eventually took over both halves after disputes arising from inaccurate estimates and calculations made by George Stephenson. The line was opened throughout, with great public rejoicing, in 1837. Passengers and mails, however, during the early days, had to change in the forecourt of Birmingham station (Curzon Street) to horse-drawn coaches.

Despite an attempted alliance it was found impossible for the steam railway and horse-drawn coach to exist in harmony. The modern form of transport was bound to predominate and before long surveys were also invited for a railway link between London and Birmingham. By May 1830 the choice lay between two routes, one through Coventry and Rugby and the other

Curzon Street Station, Birmingham, where Stephenson's London and Birmingham Railway joined with Joseph Locke's Grand Junction Railway.

through Banbury. The Stephensons were called upon to make a decision and chose the line via Coventry but with changes and modifications at the London end. Although the contract was finally awarded to 'George Stephenson and Son', there was a clear understanding between them that Robert should be Engineer-in-Chief, the duties of his father limited to work on the survey and paternal advice. Robert made sure that his would be the last word in all vital decisions, thus avoiding the complications that bedevilled the earlier construction of the Liverpool and Manchester Railway. This was to be the most ambitious railway project then planned, roundly opposed by various interests including the canal companies, stage-coach owners and many wealthy landlords who feared a trunk route might interfere with their sporting rights. Although passed by the House of Commons on 19th June 1832, it was thrown out by the Lords, almost as a matter of course. The hard-won battles of public meetings and committee rooms now seemed to have been fought in vain, with over £32,000 spent on legal and parliamentary fees alone.

Robert was at first greatly depressed but cheered by the friendly advice of Lord Wharncliffe, who advised him not to take the decision to heart. In the words of his lordship, who had served on the innumerable committees: 'The decision is against you; but you have made such a display of power that your fortune is made for life.' During the following session of Parliament, however, the bill passed with only limited opposition in either House, the London and Birmingham company having agreed to pay £750,000 for land officially valued at £250,000. This was granted the royal assent and passed into law on 6th May 1833, but it was not until 20th September that Robert Stephenson was invited to add his signature to the contract.

THE LONDON AND BIRMINGHAM RAILWAY

There had been nothing comparable to the London and Birmingham Railway since the age of the pyramids, not even the great canal projects of the late eighteenth and early nineteenth centuries. The Grand Junction Railway had been planned over a slightly shorter but much easier route. Even today the tunnels and cuttings of the line between London and Birmingham are among the most stupendous engineering works of the national system, constructed almost entirely by human labour and ingenuity. Each part of the line was divided into districts under the care of an assistant engineer, as listed below:
1. Camden Town—Aldbury (J.Birkenshaw)
2. Tring—Castlethorpe (J.Crossley)
3. Blisworth—Kilsby (F.Foster)
4. Rugby—Birmingham (T.Gooch)

Foster was later replaced by G.H.Phipps and transferred to number 4 district, Gooch having left to take charge of engineering works on the new Leeds and Manchester Railway. Robert Stephenson was responsible for the extension from Camden to Euston ratified by an act of Parliament dated 3rd July 1833. Each district was let out to small contractors, there being no large contracting firms at that time equal to coping with the line throughout. Larger projects such as tunnels and viaducts were usually let out as separate or special contracts. During the making of the line—work which continued throughout the exceptionally hard winter of 1833-34—Robert Stephenson claimed to have walked the entire length no less than fifteen times, which totalled in the region of 1,700 miles.

The first problem encountered was to gain control of land at the London end, especially in the outer suburbs, a move strongly resisted by owners of highly profitable market gardens.

The extension to a proposed terminus near Euston Square involved use of a steep incline from the station to Camden locomotive sheds, controlled during the early days of less powerful locomotives by fixed engines. Between Camden Town and Euston the line was guarded by high retaining walls with room for two double tracks. It may be noted that Euston was originally considered as a possible joint station to be shared with the proposed Bristol Railway, which later became the Great Western system. At first the retaining walls cracked and gave way in several places, due to the expansion of the local blue clay when exposed to warmth and air. Rebuilding, especially in the area of Primrose Hill Tunnel, with increased thickness of brickwork and the introduction of inverts (reversed and strengthened arches), led to estimated costs being more than doubled on this section alone. Primrose Hill Tunnel was 3,493 feet long, with ornamental portals designed by the architect W.H.Budden. Watford Tunnel, the second longest on the line, was next constructed at 5,374 feet, costing £140,000.

The embankments and cuttings, much in evidence on the central and southern portions of the line, were constructed by using what were known as 'horse runs'. This meant that a cart-horse at the top of the bank was harnessed to a large barrow of earth by a length of rope over a pulley, guided up a steep plankway by the labourer in charge. An irregular movement on the part of the horse could pitch both man and barrow down the slope at the risk of life or limb. There were up to forty horse runs at Tring alone and it is remarkable that there were few serious accidents. The men became both daring and sure-footed, although it was thought that each man must have fallen off the plankway several times a month. After a fatal accident in which a loaded barrow fell on top of a man Robert Stephenson designed a moving platform worked by machinery, but this was wrecked by workmen who considered 'it was designed to lessen their labour and wages'.

The main viaduct on the line was at Wolverton, spanning a gap in an embankment which ran across the Ouse valley for 1½ miles at an average height of 48 feet. The viaduct had six major arches of 60 foot span and 46 foot height, from crown to ground level.

One of the most serious obstacles on the route was the construction of Roade Cutting near Blisworth,

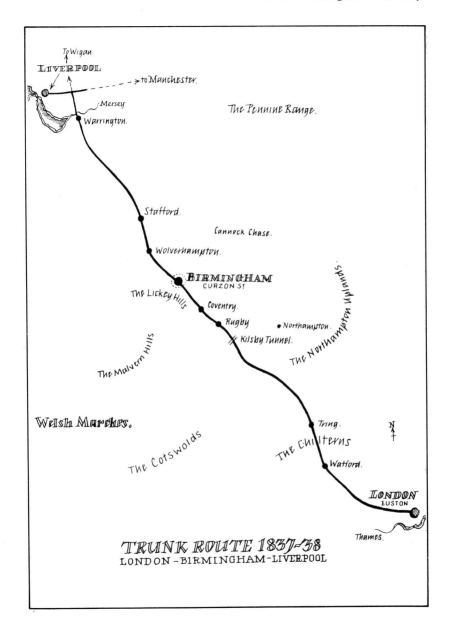

To Wigan.
LIVERPOOL
to Manchester.
The Pennine Range.
Mersey
Warrington.
Stafford.
Cannock Chase.
Wolverhampton.
BIRMINGHAM
CURZON ST
The Lickey Hills
Coventry.
The Northampton Uplands
Rugby
Northampton.
Kilsby Tunnel.
The Malvern Hills
Welsh Marches.
Tring.
N
The Chilterns
The Cotswolds
Watford.
LONDON
EUSTON
Thames.

TRUNK ROUTE 1837-38
LONDON - BIRMINGHAM - LIVERPOOL

27

Illustrations from 'Drawings of the London and Birmingham Railway' by
J. C. Bourne, published in 1839, show (top left) the oblique or skew
bridge at Boxmoor, (bottom left) the horse runs at Tring Cutting, (top

right) the building of the embankment at Wolverton, and (bottom right)
the pumping engines above the tunnel workings at Kilsby. These worked
continuously for nineteen months draining the quicksands.

Northamptonshire, sometimes known as Blisworth Cutting. This was made through crumbling oolite and clay loosened by the action of underground springs. Thick retaining walls had to be used as a means of underpinning decayed rock while costly pumping operations greatly added to overall expenditure. The final cutting was 1½ miles in length with a maximum depth of 65 feet. Over one million cubic yards of soil and clay were removed during construction. Total cost was £220,000, nearly double the original estimates.

Yet even the difficulties at Roade and Tring were minor compared with those at Kilsby Tunnel, this being the last major work on the line to be completed. Here again the main trouble lay in coping with treacherous springs, eventually overcome by the excavation of driftways or side drains. Even these proved vulnerable and just when it was thought the problem had been solved the main driftway collapsed due to encroachments from unsuspected quicksands. To master the quicksands, in turn fed by underground streams and what amounted to a subterranean lake, Robert Stephenson employed thirteen pumping engines on Kilsby Hill. These worked night and day for over nineteen months, pumping many thousands of gallons before the liquid sand was checked. The original contractor for this part of the line suffered a total breakdown of mental and physical health and died; so Robert Stephenson took personal control of the tunnel work, employing 1,300 men, 200 horses and 12 steam engines. It took over 2½ years to complete the task at a cost of between £300,000 and £400,000. The total length was 7,326 feet with two main ventilation shafts of 60 foot diameter, one being 130 feet deep. Soil excavated amounted to 177,000 cubic yards, while thirty million engineering bricks were used for lining the interior. For a period of several months, before the tunnel and other works were completed, a connection between trains on the northern and southern sections was run by the famous coaching firm of Chaplin and Horne. A change was made at a wayside inn, known as Denbigh Hall, on Watling Street where the railway crossed the road. Here passengers were allowed five minutes to transfer themselves and their luggage from railway to road coaches, the departures of which were timed to a second. Connections were made with trains at Rugby after a coach ride via Towcester, Daventry and Dunchurch, lasting upwards of three hours.

Euston Station from Bourne's 'Drawings of the London and Birmingham Railway' shows the Doric arch sadly demolished during the reconstruction of the station.

Nearing the completion of the line a celebration dinner was held at the Dun Cow, Dunchurch, on the night of 23rd December 1837. Both Robert and George Stephenson were guests of honour and during the course of the dinner Robert was presented with an engraved silver soup tureen, to which members of the staff and friends of the railway had subscribed.

The full engineering staff was present, some members having travelled well over a hundred miles to attend the function. The chair for the opening celebrations was taken by Francis Forster with George seated at his left hand and Robert at his right. Applause which greeted the combined healths of father and son was almost deafening, while everyone spoke 'with feelings that came directly from the heart'. According to the correspondent of the *Railway Times:* 'The youngest man who sat down to dinner . . . will never live to see such another day.'

Although normally a temperate man it was past 2.00 a.m. when Robert left the table accompanied by his friend Francis Forster. George was then voted into the chair but gave way to Tom Gooch shortly after 4.00 a.m. The party did not break up until six in the morning, having begun with a reception at 5.30 the previous afternoon. Some of the more hardened guests were still talking and drinking at 8.00 a.m.

The line was officially opened to through traffic—end to end—on 17th September 1838, four years after the first cutting of sods in the region of Chalk Farm (London). The actual cost was £2,400,456 or £50,000 per mile, although it was impossible to calculate the cost in terms of human suffering caused by accident, injury and death, especially in completing the larger works at Kilsby, Tring and Blisworth.

Due to a clause in the contract forming a protection against monopolies the Stephensons were not allowed to supply the line with a stud of locomotives, apart from those used in construction work. This led the London and Birmingham company to use inferior machines for several years, ordered from the Liverpool engineering firm of Bury and Company. The Forth Street works, however, continued to flourish with mounting orders from all parts of the world. Locomotives were sent to France, Russia, Germany, Italy and Belgium, to name but a few countries listed in the order book.

One of the outstanding innovations on the London to Birmingham line was the skew bridge, not previously used on railway systems in any part of the country. In the type designed by Robert Stephenson each course of masonry formed the thread of a screw, its pitch depending on angles formed by the intersection of the road and railway, affecting the radius of the arch. Final measurements were worked out on wooden models to be transferred to the prototype by means of a flexible straight edge, specially designed for the purpose.

The line was so progressive in many ways that it is strange to note the extent to which both fish-bellied and parallel or straight-sided rails were originally used, when they were already being superseded in other parts of the country by 'bullhead' rails, even on the Grand Junction line. Parallel rails weighed either 75 or 65 pounds while 'fish-bellies' weighed 50 pounds. Both wooden sleepers and stone blocks were used although mainly the latter. Stone blocks, ordered by weight, were 152,460 tons at a cost of £180,000. Rails represented 35,000 tons of iron at a cost of £460,000. Parallel rail sections were connected by means of joint chairs, replaced by fishplates after the company had been absorbed into the LNWR in 1853.

DISAPPOINTMENTS AND FRUSTRATIONS

Despite his notable success in completing the London to

Birmingham Railway, Robert Stephenson was defeated in tendering for the construction of a line between London and Brighton. This was at least partly due to his father's appearance as a supporting witness at a public hearing in this connection, the older man suffering from an unfortunate lapse of memory concerning place names. Skilful lawyers for the opposition exploited this weakness in order to discredit the scheme. By a strange coincidence the tender was eventually awarded to John Rennie, a rival of long standing, who had made the unsuccessful survey of the London to Birmingham route via Banbury.

The greatest tragedy of Robert Stephenson's life was the incurable cancer that undermined the health of his wife for a number of years, and the fact that she was unable to bear him children. Fanny Stephenson endured her sufferings with great calm and fortitude, making a peaceful end in October 1842. She begged her husband, almost on her deathbed, to marry again, but he was so attached to her memory that he was unable to think of a second marriage.

This period of his life was a chapter of accidents and misfortunes. Moving to a new house nearer his Westminster office, he was involved in a fire that destroyed a considerable amount of property, works of art and treasured personal effects.

Through no fault of his own he was later involved in the costly Stanhope and Tyne Railway fiasco, a concern for which he had agreed to act as engineer and consultant in 1832. This was a mineral line in the Pennine uplands connecting several lime works and collieries, but which did not live up to its earlier promise. As it depended for operation on the local custom of wayleave over private land it was not fully incorporated as a railway company, but was bound to strict rules of upkeep and maintenance even when it could not show a profit. Robert Stephenson had accepted a shareholding in the firm in place of a salary but was also involved, after a lapse of several years, in its burden of insolvency. To meet the claims of creditors and assist in forming a new company on the correct legal basis Robert had to contribute £20,000 of his hard-earned fortune. To round off the figure he was even forced to sell half his interest in Robert Stephenson and Company to his father. Transformed from the Stanhope and Tyne to the Pontop and South Shields Railway it was later absorbed into the rapidly

The High Level Bridge at Newcastle upon Tyne was formally opened by Queen Victoria in 1849.

expanding empire of the speculator George Hudson, then partly responsible for the 'railway mania' or boom of the 1840s. It was through his involvement with Hudson on this and other matters that Robert Stephenson was commissioned to superintend the building of the Newcastle and Darlington Junction Railway, and also to forge the final links in the East Coast Route then projected between London and Edinburgh.

The final features of the East Coast line were not completed until after Robert's death, but closely followed his designs. Notable structures were the High Level Bridge across the Tyne at Newcastle and the Royal Border Bridge at Berwick-on-Tweed. The former bridge was constructed on the 'bow and spring' girder principle similar to a canal crossing used on the London to Birmingham railway near Weedon in 1835. The Tyne Bridge carried both road and railway between Newcastle and Gateshead, 120 feet above the river. Weight of the ironwork was estimated at 5,000 tons. The Royal Border Bridge was a more conventional design but a highly impressive work, crossing the Tweed at 126 feet above water level. There were twenty-eight round arches of dressed stone with spans of 61 feet 6 inches each.

The Newcastle Bridge was completed with the closing of the final arch on 7th June 1849 and passed by an inspector for the Board of Trade a month later. In September the bridge was formally opened by Queen Victoria, who was so impressed by the magnificent structure that she agreed also to open the Royal Border Bridge twelve months later. It was during this period that Robert Stephenson was offered but refused a title.

Speaking at a celebration dinner in Newcastle shortly after the opening of the Tyne Bridge, Robert spoke with a modesty and sincerity that underlined his scorn of public honours. His words on this occasion are quoted as follows: 'If you would read the biographies of all your old distinguished engineers, you would be struck with the excessive detail into which they were drawn; when intelligence was not so widely diffused as at present, an engineer like Smeaton or Brindley had not only to conceive the design, but had to invent the machines and carry out every detail of the conception; but since then a change has taken place, and no change is more complete. The principal engineer now only has to say "Let this be done!" and it is speedily accomplished, such is the immense capital, and such the resources of mind which are immediately brought into play. I have myself, within the last ten or twelve years, done little more than exercise a general superintendence and there are many other persons here to whom the works referred to by the Chairman ought to be almost entirely attributed. I have had little or nothing to do with many of them beyond giving my name, and exercising a gentle control in some of the principal works.'

THE BATTLE OF THE GAUGES

Another unfortunate setback, this time to pride rather than pocket, was the great railway duel fought between the Stephensons and Isambard Kingdom Brunel, hoping to determine which of the railway gauges might be accepted as standard throughout the country and perhaps the world. The Stephensons—father and son—in common with other North

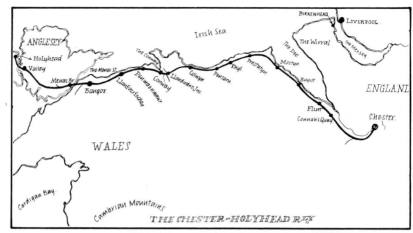

THE CHESTER–HOLYHEAD R^{LY}

Country engineers supported the narrow gauge of 4 feet 8½ inches, later to become the 'standard gauge', merely because it had been the width of earlier wagon ruts and plateways—representing the distance between the wheels of vehicles using them. In constructing the Great Western Railway Brunel had designed the seven-foot or 'broad gauge', which he felt sure would be ideal for greater loads at faster yet safer speeds. To determine the rights of the case a contest was held between chosen engines and stock of the representative railways, working over their own territories. The broad-gauge locomotive *Ixion* was declared the champion of these tests, although it is significant that it was based on a development of the earlier or 'patentee' design introduced by the Stephensons. Robert's engine was derailed at 40 miles per hour, but was acknowledged to have been an experimental long-boilered type unsuitable for express workings.

Irrespective of the outcome of these tests the broad gauge was not widely extended, except on the GWR and a few minor railways under its control. So many railways had already been constructed according to narrow-gauge specifications, while projected narrow-gauge lines were cheaper to plan and easier to construct than the more massive broad-gauge works.

Opposite: Robert Stephenson in middle age, from Jeaffreson's biography of him, published in 1864.

The tubular bridges

THE CHESTER AND HOLYHEAD RAILWAY

In June 1845 Robert Stephenson was appointed Engineer-in-Chief to the Chester and Holyhead Railway which was to be a vital link in a new crossing to Ireland, known as the 'Imperial Route'. The main problem at the outset was taking the railway across the river Conway and the more treacherous Menai Straits, obstacles that could not be avoided. Telford, the great road and canal engineer, had already spanned both places with suspension bridges but after the failure of a similar bridge designed for railway traffic at Stockton-on-Tees, this idea was abandoned. Low-slung bridges were out of the question, as were those with masonry arches, on account of the navigational requirements of the Board of Admiralty.

Yet before Robert Stephenson could master these problems of design he was affected by a great setback in the collapse of his skew bridge at Chester, forming the first part of the Chester and Holyhead contract. The bridge had been opened to traffic on 20th October 1846, having undergone an inspection by Major General Pasley for the Board of Trade. It was constructed of 87 foot compound or composite girders, reinforced with wrought iron truss rods. Even before the Chester and Holyhead system was operational the Shrewsbury and Chester Railway had obtained running rights over the bridge as a short cut to the city centre. One of their passenger trains was crossing the bridge on 24th May 1847, when two girders of the third span shattered and the train plunged to a disaster in which six people were killed, including the fireman and guard, with sixteen passengers injured. At the inquiry Robert Stephenson was absolved from blame, the accident being attributed, perhaps wrongly, to a breaking wheel which derailed the train and inflicted heavy blows on the supporting girders. Considerable doubt, however, was cast on the findings of the court and before the end of his life Robert Stephenson was fully prepared to admit that error lay with his design and the use of composite girders in general.

The tubular bridge across the Conway river was opened in 1848.

Stephenson's Britannia Tubular Bridge over the Menai Straits was opened in 1850. The central pier rests on the Britannia rock.

Other bridges of similar construction were modified or re-examined and strengthened. The idea of using cast and wrought iron together was abandoned and even cast iron was seldom used thereafter for bridging contracts.

Despite early disappointments at Chester and the spate of unwelcome publicity, many claiming that he was guilty of manslaughter through neglect, Robert Stephenson felt obliged to continue research for the projected Menai crossing, if only to restore self-confidence and vindicate himself in the eyes of the public. He eventually conceived the idea of tubular wrought iron spans, each constructed to resemble a hollow cylinder, supported on piers of masonry. Experiments to perfect the design were conducted with scale models in the shipyards of William Fairbairn and Company at Millbank, London, at a cost of £10,000. The finished tubes—to be constructed on the shores of the straits—were to carry two lines of railway across the water 1,511 feet from the Caernarvonshire shore to Anglesey, a central pier resting on the Britannia Rock, which gave its name to the finished structure. Each tube was 1,500 feet long, 23 feet deep at either end and 30 feet deep in the centre. Conway was to have a similar but smaller bridge, parallel with the earlier

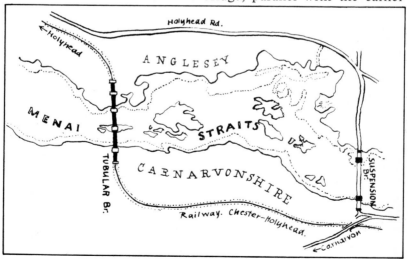

Stephenson's railway bridge crossed the Menai Straits south of and parallel to Telford's 1826 road suspension bridge.

40

Constructing one of the Britannia tubes on the shores of the Menai Straits.

Telford road bridge, and having a span of 400 feet. About 900 tons of rivet iron were used in the Menai Bridge alone.

After a successful rehearsal with the smaller Conway structure, which was opened to single line traffic in May 1848, preparations were made for raising the tubes at Menai. This was done, as at Conway, by using pontoons and hydraulic presses which raised the tubes into position, aided by the rising tide and lifting gear within the tower-like structures of the stone piers. After several accidents involving loss of human life; the destruction of valuable machinery and massive repair work, the Britannia Bridge was opened to public traffic on 18th March 1850. Total cost was in the region of £500,000, a large proportion of which was contributed by the London and Birmingham Railway Company, as the new link via Holyhead was expected to greatly increase traffic over their lines from both London and the Midlands; all parts of the system were eventually absorbed by the London and North Western company.

The sides and top of the Britannia Bridge tubes were lined with wooden beams, which served as a form of insulation. In the days of steam, drivers were instructed to cut off steam at the approaches to the bridge and there were also speed restrictions. On 23rd May 1970, trespassers accidentally set fire to the interior of the bridge, which was so badly damaged that the line remained closed for twenty months. During this period damaged tubes were replaced by steel arches, although the original stone piers have been retained. The new bridge is for single traffic only. This was not the only damage caused by accident as a less serious fire had been started by a painter's blowlamp in June 1946. This was soon brought under control but the driver of the down Irish Mail, unable to stop, was forced to accelerate to safety through a wall of flames.

A further important feature of the Chester to Holyhead line was the artificial terrace cut for the sole use of the railway round the sea-girt headland of Penmaenmawr. Nearly midway between Conway and Bangor, this consisted of a mountain with precipitous sides jutting into the Irish Sea and frequently assailed by winter storms. A sea wall had to be built in certain parts while in others the terrace was blasted directly from the foot of the rocks. The terrace began on the Conway side of the mountain with a tunnel of 10½ chains through the actual headland, continuing beyond the further tunnel mouth for 1¼ miles, interrupted by three short embankments. In certain places the terrace and embankments were protected from rock falls by a covered way or shelter. While the sea-wall was being constructed an unexpected spring tide of 17 feet combined with a south-westerly gale to wreck most of the finished work. Two hundred yards of sea-wall were later replaced by a viaduct of cast iron girders, the piers of which faced edgeways to the sea, with ten horizontal girders of 42 foot lengths. Further damage was later sustained on other parts of the wall and terrace, which led to a complete reorganisation of the contract. Massive outworks were constructed including protective piles to break the force of incoming waves, especially where there had been a threatened breach. The time taken in constructing this part of the line was in the region of three years.

CONTRACTS ABROAD

Following the success of the Menai and Conway tubular bridges two similar structures were erected in Egypt, one spanning the Nile at Benha and the other crossing the Karineen Canal. Both the Egyptian bridges had swing sections for the through navigation of shipping and were opened to public traffic in the autumn of 1855.

A fifth tubular bridge of Robert Stephenson's design, now

On the Chester to Holyhead line, Stephenson had difficulty skirting the Penmaenmawr headland and at one place a viaduct was built over the sea. This part of the line took three years to complete.

superseded, was built to span the St. Lawrence at Montreal, where the river was nearly two miles across. Stephenson went to Canada to survey the site for the 'Victoria Bridge' and make plans, which were carried out by the British contractors Thomas Brassey and Messrs Peto and Betts, working in partnership. The main structure, consisted of twenty-five sections supported on twenty-four piers. Two central navigation spans had a high water-level clearance of 30 feet, rising to 60 feet. Most of the ironwork was prepared in England, marked out and drilled under the personal supervision of Robert Stephenson, and shipped to the St. Lawrence from Birkenhead. The first train ran across the bridge six weeks after the death of its designer.

In 1845 Robert Stephenson had been invited to plan and supervise the construction of a railway line in Norway between Christiania and Lake Miosen. He began the survey in 1850 and paid several visits to the line in 1845, 1850, 1851, 1852 and 1854. During his absence he was represented by G.P.Bidder,

The Victoria Bridge across the St. Lawrence at Montreal in Canada was Stephenson's fifth tubular design. Most of the ironwork was prepared in England and shipped to Canada. The bridge spanned two miles of water.

acting as resident engineer. This was the first railway in Norway to serve the general public. It proved a highly popular and successful project, for which Robert was decorated with the Order of St. Olaf.

STEPHENSON'S DEATH

One of Robert Stephenson's last important works was to repair and strengthen the cast iron bridge over the river Wear at Sunderland. This was the second cast iron bridge in the world of any size or importance; the first spans the Severn at Ironbridge near Coalbrookdale in Shropshire.

Robert Stephenson died at the early age of fifty-six on 12th October 1859, returning to his deathbed in England from what should have been a holiday and rest cure in Egypt. This was not more than ten years after the death of his father. He had been worn down in body and spirit for several years and never fully recovered from the loss of his wife, to which the death of his father from a sudden lung haemorrhage added further distress. While his health was often far from perfect he had involved himself with so many schemes and projects, exposing himself to all kinds of weather, that it may be claimed with some reason that he worked himself to death. Far more than a builder of bridges and railways Robert Stephenson was a man of culture, a connoisseur of the arts, and involved in several national and political issues of his day. He sat as a Tory member of Parliament for Whitby from 1847 but was far from being a party hack, although strongly opposed to free trade. His maiden speech in favour of the Great Exhibition, found him in direct conflict with a fellow Tory, Colonel Sibthorp, an arch-enemy of the industrial revolution. At a later period he sided with the Liberal-Radical Roebuck, concerning the mismanagement of the Crimean War, which led to the defeat of the Government. For two years he was a lively president of the Institute of Mechanical Engineers, also being the first civil engineer to become a millionaire.

Awarded many honours both at home and abroad Robert Stephenson refused a knighthood and would not allow his foreign titles and decorations to be recognised in England. He was an eminently clubbable man and enjoyed dining out and entertaining in his own home. Towards the end of his life, however, it may be felt that the need for company was partly to assuage his feelings of loss and introspection. Moderate in the pleasures of the table his main weakness was a love of strong cigars, although in order to ease the tension of difficult work he also came to rely, to a limited extent, on tranquillising drugs. Although modest and charming amongst his friends, he lacked the hearty, robust character of his father and has been criticised for a dearth of the humour and spontaneity so much appreciated in a public figure. Yet it is as an engineer and organiser of vast projects that he should be finally judged. Although not without faults and guilty of several serious errors, many of his chief works still stand in daily use, witness to his energy, inventiveness and faith in human progress.

At the death of Robert Stephenson the whole nation was plunged into mourning. As a mark of respect his body was laid beside the remains of Thomas Telford in the nave of Westminster Abbey. The funeral cortége was given royal permission—a rare privilege—to pass through Hyde Park, along a route lined with silent crowds. All shipping in the Thames lowered its flags to half mast, while business and trade in Newcastle were suspended on the day of the funeral. So passed one of the greatest engineers of all time, honoured not only by men of power and rank but by the unaspiring—craftsmen and labourers—who helped to construct the great railway systems he envisaged. He never rose high enough to forget his own early struggle and humble origins and was always glad to acknowledge the debt of gratitude owed to friends, assistants and collaborators. He was of a forgiving nature and on the best of terms with those with whom he had formerly been in conflict, including Isambard Kingdom Brunel. He died slightly less than a month after Brunel and was only three years his senior.

It was the end of a great era.

BIBLIOGRAPHY

Lives of the Engineers (Vol. 3) Samuel Smiles (John Murray) 1862. Reprinted with introduction by L. T. C. Rolt (David and Charles) 1968.

The Life of George Stephenson Samuel Smiles (John Murray) 1864.

The Life of Robert Stephenson J. C. Jeaffreson (Longmans, Green) 1864.

British Engineers Metius Chapell (Collins) 1942.

The Railway Engineers O. S. Nock (Batsford) 1955.

George and Robert Stephenson L. T. C. Rolt (Longmans) 1960.

Liverpool Road Station, Manchester, is now part of the Greater Manchester Museum of Science and Industry. This photograph shows the Station Agent's House (1806) and the First Class Passenger Booking Hall (1830), both restored to their original appearance.

THE PRINCIPAL EVENTS OF STEPHENSON'S LIFE

1803   Robert Stephenson born

1804   *Trevithick's Penydaren locomotive*

1815   Attends the Academy of Dr Bruce

1819   Apprenticed to Nicholas Wood at Killingworth Colliery

1821   Worked with his father, George Stephenson, on survey for Stockton and Darlington Railway

1823   Opening of the Forth Street Works, Newcastle

1824   Appointed to control of mining operations in Colombia, South America

1825   Opening of Stockton and Darlington Railway

1826   *Telford's Menai Bridge opened*

1827   Leaves South America to resume control at Forth Street

1829   Work on Canterbury and Whitstable and Leicester and Swannington railways. Marries Fanny Sanderson. *Rocket* wins premier award at Rainhill Trials

1830   Opening of the Canterbury and Whitstable Railway. Opening of the Liverpool and Manchester Railway.

1833   Act of Parliament for the London and Birmingham Railway

1837   Opening of the Grand Junction Railway

1838   Opening of the London and Birmingham Railway

1841   *Brunel completes the Great Western Railway*

1845   Appointed Engineer-in-Chief to the Chester-Holyhead Railway. Invited to build railway in Norway

1846   Commenced work on tubular bridges at Conway and Menai Straits (Britannia Bridge)

1847   Elected M.P. for Whitby. Collapse of the Dee Bridge at Chester

1849   Opening of the High Level Bridge, Newcastle, and the Conway Tubular Bridge

1850   Opening of the Britannia Tubular Bridge, and the Royal Border Bridge

1853   Completed work on Norwegian Railway between Christiana and Lake Miosen. Decorated with Norwegian Order of St.Olaf

1854   Work commenced on the Victoria Tubular Bridge, Montreal

1855   Opening of two Nile bridges for the Alexandria and Cairo Railway

1859   Stephenson dies. *Brunel dies*

INDEX

Page numbers in italic refer to illustrations